MASTERING YOUR FEELINGS AND EMOTIONS:

A Guide to Handling Feelings and Managing your Emotions

Ella Morris

Table of Contents

CHAPTER 1

Emotions play a key part in our lives since they have essential purposes. This module explains such functions, splitting the subject into three areas: the intrapersonal, the interpersonal, and the societal and cultural functions of emotions.

The section on the intrapersonal functions of emotion describes the roles that emotions play within each of us individually; the section on the interpersonal functions of emotion describes the meanings of emotions to our relationships with others, and the section on the social and cultural functions of emotion describes the roles and meanings that emotions have to the maintenance and effective functioning of our societies and cultures at large.

All in all, we shall see that emotions are a vitally significant component of our psychological makeup, having significance and purpose to each of us individually, in our connections with others in groups, and to our society as a whole.

It is difficult to fathom living without feeling. We appreciate our feelings—the thrill at a ball game, the pleasure of the touch of a loved one, or the fun with friends on a night out. Even negative emotions are significant, such as the grief when a loved one dies, the wrath when violated, the fear that fills us in a dangerous or unexpected scenario, or the guilt or humiliation toward others when our transgressions are made public.

Emotions color life events and give those encounters significance and flavor.

In truth, emotions play many significant roles in people's lives and have been the object of scientific investigation in psychology for well over a century. This session addresses why we have emotions and why they are essential. Doing so requires us to understand the function of emotions, and this module does so below by dividing the discussion into three sections. The first addresses the intrapersonal functions of emotion, which allude to the role that emotions play inside each of us personally.

The second involves the interpersonal functions of emotion, which allude to the role emotions play between people within a group. The third involves the social and cultural functions of emotion, which allude to the role that emotions play in the preservation of social order within a community.

All in all, we shall see that emotions tell us who we are, what our connections with others are like, and how to behave in social interactions. Emotions provide meaning to events; without emotions, such occurrences would be simple facts. Emotions help manage interpersonal connections. And emotions play a crucial part in the cultural functioning of keeping human communities together.

Intrapersonal Functions of Emotion

Emotions Help us Act Quickly with Minimal Conscious Awareness

Emotions are quick information-processing systems that enable us to behave with minimum thought. Challenges connected with birth, conflict, death, and seduction have happened throughout evolutionary history, and emotions developed to enable people to react to those problems fast and with minimum conscious cognitive involvement.

If we did not have emotions, we could not make swift judgments about whether to fight, defend, run, care for others, refuse food, or approach something helpful, all of which were functionally adapted in our evolutionary past and allowed us to live.

For instance, drinking spoilt milk or eating rotting eggs has bad repercussions for human wellness. The sense of revulsion, however, enables us instantly take action by avoiding eating them in the first place or by vomiting them out. This reaction is adaptive since it benefits, eventually, in our survival and enables us to respond promptly without much thought.

In certain circumstances, having the time to sit and calmly think about what to do, calculating cost-benefit ratios in one's thoughts, is a luxury that can cost one's life. Emotions developed so that we may behave without that level of reasoning.

Emotions Prepare the Body for Immediate Action

Emotions prepare us for conduct. When triggered, emotions orchestrate systems such as perception, attention, inference, learning, memory, goal choice, motivational priorities, physiological reactions, motor behaviors, and behavioral decision making. Emotions concurrently activate some systems and deactivate others to avoid the chaos of competing systems working at the same time, allowing for coordinated reactions to external inputs.

For instance, when we are terrified, our systems shut down momentarily unwanted digestion processes, resulting in saliva decrease (a dry mouth); blood rushes disproportionately to the bottom half of the body; the visual field expands, and the air is sucked in, all preparing the body to leave.

Emotions originate from a system of components that encompasses subjective experience, expressive behaviors, physiological responses, behavioral inclinations, and cognition, all for the goals of particular activities; the name "emotion" is, in actuality, a metaphor for these reactions.

One typical misperception many people have when thinking about emotions, however, is the assumption that emotions must always immediately create action. This is not true.

Emotion prepares the body for action; however, whether individuals engage in action is based on numerous aspects, such as the environment within which the emotion has happened, the target of the emotion, the anticipated repercussions of one's actions, past experiences, and so forth. Thus, emotions are merely one of many drivers of behavior, although a significant one.

Emotions Influence Thoughts

Emotions are also tied to ideas and memories. Memories are not only facts that are recorded in our brains; they are tinted with the emotions felt at those moments the facts happened. Thus, emotions serve as the neural glue that connects those disparate facts in our minds. That is why it is easier to recall good ideas while joyful, and angry moments when furious.

Emotions serve as the affective foundation of many attitudes, values, and beliefs that we have about the world and the people around us; without emotions, such attitudes, values, and beliefs would be mere assertions without meaning, and emotions give those statements meaning.

Emotions impact our mental processes, sometimes in beneficial ways, sometimes not. It is difficult to think critically and clearly when we experience powerful emotions, but easier when we are not overwhelmed by emotions.

Emotions Motivate Future Behaviors

Because emotions prepare our bodies for imminent action, impact thinking, and can be felt, they are essential motivators of future conduct. Many of us try to experience the sensations of satisfaction, pleasure, pride, or victory in our successes and achievements.

At the same time, we also work very hard to avoid strong negative feelings; for example, once we have felt the emotion of disgust when drinking spoiled milk, we generally work very hard to avoid having those feelings again (e.g., checking the expiration date on the label before buying the milk, smelling the milk before drinking it, watching if the milk curdles in one's coffee before drinking it). Emotions, therefore, not only affect current acts but also serve as a key motivating foundation for future behaviors.

Interpersonal Functions of Emotion

Emotions are communicated both orally via words and nonverbally through facial expressions, voices, gestures, body postures, and movements. We are continually displaying emotions while dealing with others, and others can accurately interpret such emotional manifestations; consequently, emotions signal value to others and impact others and our social relationships.

Emotions and their manifestations send information to others about our sentiments, goals, connection with the target of the emotions, and the surroundings. Because emotions have this communicative signal value, they assist solve social issues by inspiring reactions from others, communicating the nature of interpersonal connections, and by offering incentives for desirable social behaviors.

Emotional Expressions Facilitate Specific Behaviors in Perceivers

Because facial expressions of emotion are universal social signals, they include significance not just about the expresser's psychological state but also about that person's purpose and future action. This knowledge impacts what the perceiver is likely to do.

Persons watching terrified expressions, for instance, are more likely to create approach-related behaviors, while people who observe furious faces are more likely to produce avoidance-related behaviors. Even subliminal display of smiles generates increases in how much beverage individuals pour and drink and how much they are ready to pay for it; the presentation of angry expressions diminishes these actions.

Also, emotional displays evoke specific, complementary emotional responses from observers; for example, anger evokes fear in others, whereas distress evokes sympathy and aid.

Emotional Expressions Signal the Nature of Interpersonal Relationships

Emotional expressions convey information about the nature of the connections among interactants. Some of the most significant and startling set of results in this field comes from research involving married couples.

In this study, married couples attended a laboratory after having not seen each other for 24 hours, and then participated in personal dialogues about everyday happenings or topics of contention. Discrete displays of scorn, particularly by the males, and disgust, mainly by the women, predicted subsequent marital discontent and even divorce.

Emotional Expressions Provide Incentives for Desired Social Behavior

Facial expressions of emotion are essential regulators of social interaction. In the developmental literature, this topic has been examined under the concept of social reference; that is, the process whereby babies seek out information from others to explain a situation and then utilize that knowledge to behave.

By far, the greatest example of social reference comes from studies on the visual cliff. In the first study to investigate this concept, Campos and colleagues placed mothers on the far end of the "cliff" from the infant. Mothers initially smiled at the newborns and put a toy on top of the safety glass to lure them; infants inevitably started crawling to their mothers.

When the newborns were in the middle of the table, however, the mother then presented an emotion of fear, grief, anger, curiosity, or excitement. The findings were different for the various faces; no newborn crossed the table when the mother displayed fear; just 6% did when the mother presented anger, 33% crossed when the mother projected grief and nearly 75% of the babies crossed when the mother posed pleasure or curiosity.

Other research gives comparable evidence for facial expressions as controllers of social interaction. In one research, experimenters presented facial expressions of neutral, anger, or disgust at newborns as they advanced toward an item and examined the level of inhibition the babies displayed in touching the object.

The findings for 10- and 15-month-olds were the same: anger induced the highest inhibition, followed by disgust, with neutral the least. This research was then duplicated using pleasure and disgust emotions, changing the approach such that the babies were not permitted to touch the toy (compared with a distractor item) until one hour following exposure to the expression.

At 14 months of age, considerably more babies touched the toy when they witnessed cheerful emotions, but fewer touched the item when the infants saw displeasure.

Social and Cultural Functions of Emotion

If you pause to think about many things we take for granted in our everyday lives, we cannot help but come to the conclusion that contemporary human existence is a colorful tapestry of numerous groups and individual lives are woven together in a complicated but useful fashion.

For example, when you're hungry, you might go to the local grocery store and buy some food. Ever stop to think about how you're able to do that? You may purchase a banana that was cultivated in a field in southeast Asia being farmed by farmers there, where they planted the tree, cared for it, and gathered the fruit. They presumably passed that fruit over to a distribution network that enabled several individuals somewhere to utilize things such as cranes, vehicles, cargo bins, ships, or aircraft (that were also manufactured by many people somewhere) to transport that banana to your shop.

The business has workers to care for the banana till you arrived and grabbed it and bargain with you for it (with your money). You may have come to the shop on a vehicle that was made someplace else in the globe by others, and you were presumably wearing clothing produced by some other people somewhere else.

Thus, human social existence is complicated. Individuals are members of several groups, with different social roles, norms, and expectations, and they move swiftly in and out of the multiple groups of which they are members. Moreover, much of human social activity is unusual because it focuses on cities, where many individuals of diverse origins come together. This generates the immense potential for social disorder, which may easily arise if people are not coordinated properly and connections were not managed methodically.

One of the key responsibilities of culture is to give this required coordination and order. Doing so allows individuals and groups to negotiate the social complexity of human social life, thereby maintaining social order and preventing social chaos.

Culture does this by providing a meaning and information system to its members, which is shared by a group and transmitted across generations, that allows the group to meet basic needs of survival, pursue happiness and well-being, and derive meaning from life. Culture is what allowed the banana from southeast Asia to appear on your table.

Cultural transmission of the meaning and information system to its members is, therefore, a crucial aspect of culture. One of the ways this transmission happens is via the formation of worldviews (including attitudes, values, beliefs, and norms) associated with told emotions.

Worldviews connected to emotions give recommendations for desired feelings that support rules for managing individual actions and interpersonal relationships. Our cultural roots teach us which emotions are desirable to have, and which are not. The cultural transmission of knowledge connected to emotions happens in numerous ways, from childrearers to children, as well as via the cultural items accessible in our environments, such as books, movies, advertising, and the likes.

Cultures also instruct us on what to do with our emotions—that is, how to regulate or change them—when we encounter them. One of the ways in which this is done is via the regulation of our emotional expressions through cultural display guidelines.

These are guidelines that are learned early in life that define the control and alteration of our emotional manifestations according to social conditions. Thus, we learn that “big guys don’t cry” or to laugh at the boss’s jokes even when they’re not humorous. By altering how individuals express their emotions, culture also impacts how people feel them as well.

Because one of the major functions of culture is to maintain social order to ensure group efficiency and thus survival, cultures create worldviews, rules, guidelines, and norms concerning emotions because emotions have important intra- and interpersonal functions, as described above, and are important motivators of behavior. Norms surrounding emotion and its control in all cultures serve the objective of sustaining social order.

Cultural worldviews and norms assist us in regulating and changing our emotional responses (and consequently behaviors) by enabling us to have specific sorts of emotional experiences in the first place and by regulating our emotions and subsequent behaviors after we have them.

By doing so, our culturally moderated emotions can help us engage in socially appropriate behaviors, as defined by our cultures, and thus reduce social complexity and increase social order, avoiding social chaos.

All of this helps us to live reasonably peaceful and useful lives in groups. If cultural worldviews and norms regarding emotions did not exist, individuals would run wild experiencing all kinds of emotional experiences, expressing their feelings, and then acting in all sorts of unanticipated and sometimes destructive ways.

If such were the case, it would be extremely impossible for groups and societies to operate successfully, and even for humans to live as a species, if emotions were not controlled in culturally determined ways for the common, social good. Thus, emotions play a key part in the effective functioning of every community and civilization.

CHAPTER 2

Healthy emotional development is marked by a gradually increasing ability to perceive, assess, and manage emotions. This is a biological process driven by physical and cognitive changes and heavily influenced by context and environment.

Adults sometimes expect to keep their emotions from interfering with performance in school, work, and other activities, but doing so may be challenging in a complex environment. Some people may be excited to take on new challenges as they become more independent, whereas others may need more support to build their confidence.

The process of emotional development gives young adults the opportunity to build skills, discover unique qualities, and develop strengths for optimal health.

Factors that affect how well adults navigate this process include:
1. Hormones: These critical chemicals in the brain that bring about physical changes also affect young adults' moods and heighten their emotional responses. These characteristics together mean that young adults can be swayed by emotion and have difficulty making decisions that adults find appropriate.

2. Identity formation. There are many facets to identity formation, which include developmental tasks such as becoming independent and achieving a sense of competence. Young adults may question their passions and values, examine their relationships with family and peers, and think about their talents and definitions of success. Identity building is a cyclical process during which young adults continually experiment with various ideas, companions, and hobbies.

This exploration is typical and may afford them the opportunity to learn more about themselves and others, but it isn't necessarily paired with thinking or a cognitive capacity to understand the repercussions of their choices. Although this road to defining one's identity might be tough for some families, it also helps drive young adults to learn about themselves and grow more secure in their own, distinct identities.

3. Stress. Adults live in a variety of contexts and face a broad range of stresses that impact emotional development. Learning good reactions to stressful events is part of regular growth, and some stress may even be helpful. However, some people encounter exceptionally traumatic circumstances, such as experiencing or witnessing traumatic events.

Some people may have to cope with numerous sorts of traumatic stress. These more intense kinds of stress generally referred to as toxic stress, may impair their systems, resulting in persistent physical health issues and possibly leading to despair, anxiety, and other mental health disorders.

Toxic stress also may contribute to stress-related disorders and cognitive impairment in maturity. Adults who experience this form of stress also are more likely to use harmful substances, engage in other risky behaviors, and experience post-traumatic stress disorder (PTSD), a condition in which a person relives a traumatic event through persistent memories or flashbacks and experiences other symptoms such as insomnia, angry outbursts, or feeling tense.

However, individuals react to stress differently, and a solid support system may help shield them from long-lasting negative consequences and establish an atmosphere that allows kids to develop.

Many individuals find it challenging to convey their feelings. Some individuals overly convey what they feel, while others don't share enough. Knowing how to communicate your emotions in a precise and measured manner can benefit you enormously in your personal, social, and professional life.

There are various ideas and approaches that teach how to either suppress or regulate emotions. It has been proven though, that this approach is not effective. Emotions and sentiments are spontaneous and instinctive, they are supposed to be felt and shared.

It has been demonstrated on a scientific level that ignoring and suppressing emotions may have harmful psychological implications. Modern treatments like acceptance and commitment therapy, and other techniques like mindfulness, may assist you to accept your feelings and know how to address them. Your emotions are part of you and need to be taken care of.

For example, if you are a person who feels a lot of emotional anxiety, you may do particular things and act in a specific manner to avoid that worry. This may be because you aren't sure how to channel it and express it.

This emotional suppression may produce physical difficulties, such as a fast heartbeat, excessive perspiration, shaking, or breathing problems. When sentiments are kept back, tension is developed. This stress may be centered physically in locations like the neck, face, numerous muscles, and spine.
If, on the other hand, you hold to these feelings without expressing them, you may be subject to having psychosomatic ailments of the arteries, head pains, or stomach difficulties. It is a proven reality that your

emotions affect your physical wellbeing. Knowing how to communicate your feelings might help avoid physical ailments and mental distress.

Know how to convey your feelings

With a little bit of training and by following these basic steps, you will be able to better understand your emotions and communicate them effectively.

Below is an overview of these eleven stages so you may start to put them into practice:

Identify the emotion and the feeling:
When anything changes in your body from responding to something, either external or something inside your thoughts, you should ask yourself: What am I feeling? What physical symptoms am I experiencing? What is the cause? Why is it occurring now?

Learn to recognize your feelings:

Once you have recognized your emotions and sentiments, you have to examine the sense that it causes inside you. It is useful to recognize what indications and gestures betray you. Try to compile a note of all of those feelings and what precisely it is that physically gives them away.

Pay attention to your body's reaction:
Emotions are governed by the limbic system and the neurological system and are difficult to manage when they first occur. Take a minute and allow the emotion you are experiencing to settle so you can think properly about it, and about how you will respond to it.

Pay greater attention to how you react to a certain situation:
You may feel that the scenario is what makes you uneasy, but the basis of the issue is your emotional reaction to the event. Observe yourself and you will see that your reaction is the same as when you can't locate

an essential document, or when you are punished for a traffic infraction you didn't commit. The only thing you can alter is your response.

Express your emotions accurately and proportionally:
Once you have thoroughly mastered the previous phase, you will be able to communicate your feelings in a more controlled manner. Still, however, you may learn a few additional steps to assist you in grasping what is occurring to you so you can articulate it effectively.

Communicate with and explore your body:
When you feel these intense emotions, take notice of the portion of your body from where they arise. Give them a color and a palpable feel. Spot them in a special place and attempt to develop a new connection with them. You are that which constitutes your body and your emotions; they do not possess you.

Try to be honest about what you feel and what you do:
If, in actuality, you feel indifferent towards someone or something, why keep attempting to make it work? Or if you are upset, annoyed, and furious, why avoid a dialogue that can help you understand yourself a bit better?

Choose the finest scenario in which to express yourself:
If, for example, you have a disagreement with your employer and want to have a productive dialogue with him or her, you will do nothing if you select the incorrect time in which to do it. Therefore, consider the circumstance, the people around you, and yourself while selecting when the finest time will be.

Utilize a positive style of communication:

A nice tone, active listening, eye contact, and using simple statements like "I feel stressed" instead of "what occurred at work today made me so stressed" can help you avoid a scenario in which you need to go back and recount what happened. The other person will implicitly understand that your stress is caused by work.

Use your body to assist yourself convey what you feel:
In the process of saying that you are stressed, place your hand on your heart, on your head, or your stomach. This insinuates that you are having negative sensations and that it would be desirable for you and your surroundings to not carry on in that situation.

Visualizing and localizing your emotions is essential:
You are in control of regulating your own emotions and sentiments, without stifling them or concealing them. You need to

express them to be able to alleviate and soothe yourself and your thoughts, and so that they may be understood.

How to quiet your emotion

Sometimes emotional distress has nothing to do with an actual tangible issue. You may be sad because of things you recall, or you feel under the weather, or for any unhappy notion that may be in your thoughts. In these instances, you may use what has previously been mentioned: embrace these sensations as part of yourself. Feel the discomfort and recognize that you are a live person who should embrace such sensations.

Accepting ourselves as emotional beings is the key to being able to determine which feelings are those which we should hold on to, and which we should communicate to others.

Emotions are part of the development of humans as a species and are also what characterize and differentiate people from the rest of the creatures that occupy the world. Emotions are normal, so don't strive against them over and over again. Let them be, and in the meantime, try to relax. Find anything else to occupy your thoughts like chatting to someone, writing, or going for a stroll.

If you do encounter tremendously strong emotions like fury, consider performing an intensive sport. That will help you to relieve your bottled-up rage and tension that might build up inside.

CHAPTER 3

Enter emotional intelligence (EI), a collection of talents that enable us to perceive, understand, and control our own emotions as well as recognize, understand and impact the emotions of others.

Additionally, research reveals that persons with a high emotional quotient (EQ) are more inventive and have better work satisfaction than those with lower EQs.
Let's look into what precisely EI comprises, and how you may improve on this key component of effective relationships.

What Are the Components of Emotional Intelligence?

Emotional intelligence is a collection of abilities and behaviors. While some individuals will be innately more competent at some elements, EI may be learned, developed, and strengthened.

The four basic components of EI are self-awareness, self-regulation, social awareness, and social skills:

Self-Awareness

Self-awareness is the capacity to detect and comprehend your own emotions and the influence we have on others. It's the cornerstone of emotional intelligence and the other components of EI rely on this self-awareness.

It all begins with self-awareness, which is the cornerstone of EI, and it grows from there. If you're conscious of your own emotions and the actions they provoke, you may begin to regulate these feelings and behaviors.

Our emotions impact our mood, actions, performance, and relationships with other people. We are all experiencing emotions all the time, the problem is whether you are mindful of these feelings and the effect they have on your actions - and other people.

According to organizational psychologists, self-aware individuals tend to be more confident and more creative. They also make better judgments, develop stronger connections, and communicate more effectively.

Self-Regulation

Self-awareness opens the way to self-regulation, which is the capacity to regulate these emotions and actions. Once we're conscious of our emotions, we can begin to regulate them and keep the disruptive emotions and impulses under control.

Social Awareness

Social awareness is our capacity to comprehend the feelings of others and a fundamental component of this is empathy.

People with good social awareness are inclined toward compassion. However, this doesn't imply they cannot offer others severe criticism; they may be better at giving this 'tough love' since they understand the other person and want to help them develop.

Social Skills

Social skills are what differentiate a great manager from a decent one. These abilities, which include influence, conflict management, collaboration, and the capacity to inspire others, make it easy to develop and sustain good connections in all sectors of your life.

Others with great social skills may make a significant impact on a team and in organizations because they understand others and act on this understanding to lead people toward a shared goal.

To enhance your emotional intelligence, you need to start at the beginning, with self-awareness. However, evaluating your self-awareness is fundamentally difficult because you don't know what you don't know.

Without an objective knowledge of who you are and what motivates you, it's practically hard to be emotionally intelligent.
However, using more empirical measures of self-awareness, the research indicated that just 10-15 percent of the sample was self-aware.

That's a rather huge gap and one that shows most of us aren't particularly self-aware. What's more, research also reveals that managers and CEOs may be the least self-aware of all. This is not despite their authority, but very probably because of it.
After all, individuals at the top of the pyramid have fewer people offering them feedback.

Often, when managers do get feedback from workers, it isn't as honest as it may be because subordinates are fearful of incurring unfavorable repercussions. Managers are sheltered from criticism, and as a consequence, self-awareness declines. Receiving honest, constructive criticism is crucial to becoming self-aware.

A 360-degree emotional intelligence evaluation may be a highly effective technique to obtain insight into your EI components and the influence you have on others. Many individuals brush off variations in how they assess themselves vs how others score them on EI abilities by arguing that they're too harsh on themselves or that others don't truly grasp their intent, but it demonstrates a lack of self-awareness.

What Are the Signs of Emotional Intelligence?

Emotional intelligence is a set of skills and behaviors that can be learned and developed. Here are some telltale signs of people with low EQ and those with high EQ.

People with low EQ:
-Often feels misunderstood.
-Get upset easily and Become overwhelmed by emotions.
-Have trouble being assertive.

People with high EQ:
-Understand the links between their emotions and how they behave.
-Remain calm and composed during stressful situations
-Can inspire people toward the same aim.
-Handle tough individuals with tact and diplomacy

Three Steps Toward Improved Emotional Intelligence

Developing emotional intelligence is an ongoing process. The journey differs from person to person. The following actions may lead you to better self-awareness, empathy, and social skills.

1. Recognize your emotions and name them What emotions are you experiencing right now? Can you name them? When in a difficult circumstance, what emotions normally arise? How would you prefer to react in these situations? Can you stop to pause and evaluate your response? Taking a moment to name your feelings and temper your reactivity is an integral step toward EI.

2. Ask for feedback
Audit your self-perception by asking supervisors, coworkers, acquaintances, or family how they would grade your emotional intelligence. For example, question them about how you react to challenging circumstances, how adaptive or empathic you are, and/or how effectively you manage disagreement. It may not always be what you want to hear, but it will frequently be what you need to hear.

3. Read literature Studies suggest that reading literature with complex characters

helps boost empathy. Reading tales from other people's viewpoints helps us acquire insight into their ideas, motives, and behaviors and may help boost your social awareness.

How to Establish a Culture of Emotional Intelligence

Building E.I. in oneself is one thing, but convincing others to adopt a more empathic perspective may be a problem. To build a culture of high EQ, managers, and supervisors must model emotionally intelligent conduct.

If you want to improve how your company behaves in EI, you can define norms for how people interact and how they disagree.
In addition, you need to acknowledge and appreciate those who display emotional intelligence.

Start making heroes of people who help other people, it's not just the person who got to the top of the mountain first, it's all the people who helped them. If you want to support excellent team conduct, identify it, and call it out for what it is.

CHAPTER 4

Managing Emotions at Work

In your personal life, your response to stressful events like these may be to start yelling or to go hide in a corner and feel sorry for yourself for a bit. But at work, these forms of conduct might drastically impair your professional reputation, as well as your productivity.

Stressful scenarios are all too prevalent in a business that's suffering budget cutbacks, personnel layoffs, and department changes. It may get harder and harder to regulate your emotions under these conditions, but it's even more crucial for you to do so.

After all, if management is pressed into making additional layoffs, they may prefer to maintain individuals who can regulate their emotions, and perform effectively under pressure. No matter what the scenario is, you're always free to choose how you respond to it.

So, how can you grow better at regulating your emotions, and "choosing" your responses to negative situations? In this post, we look at the most frequent negative emotions encountered in the workplace - and how you may handle them successfully.

Why are we concentrating primarily on negative emotions? Well, most individuals don't require tactics for controlling their pleasant emotions. After all, sentiments of pleasure, enthusiasm, compassion, or optimism normally don't affect others in a bad manner. As long as you convey pleasant feelings constructively and professionally, they're fantastic to have on the job!

Common Negative Emotions at Work

-Frustration/irritation.

-Worry/nervousness.

-Anger/aggravation.

-Dislike.
-Disappointment/unhappiness.

Below are numerous ways you may take to assist you to cope with each of these bad feelings.

Frustration/Irritation

Frustration generally develops when you feel stuck or imprisoned, or unable to go ahead in some manner. It might be caused by a colleague obstructing your favorite project, a supervisor who is too unorganized to attend your meeting on time, or just being on the phone for a long period.

Whatever the reason, it's crucial to deal with feelings of annoyance swiftly, since they may easily develop into other unpleasant emotions, such as rage.

Here are some recommendations for coping with frustration:

Stop and examine - One of the finest things you can do is mentally stop yourself, and look at the circumstance. Ask yourself why you feel irritated. Write it down, and be detailed. Then think about one good thing about your present position. For instance, if your boss is late for your meeting, then you have extra time to prepare. Or, you may utilize this opportunity to rest a bit.

Find something nice about the circumstance - Thinking about a positive element of your circumstance frequently lets you look at things from a new perspective. This tiny shift in your thinking might boost your attitude. When it's individuals who are creating your irritation, they're generally not doing it purposely to bother you. And if it's a thing that's upsetting you; well, it's not personal! Don't be upset, just go on.

Remember the last time you were irritated The last time you were angry about anything, the issue probably turned out just fine after a while, right? Your sentiments of aggravation or irritation probably didn't accomplish anything to fix the situation then, which means they're not doing much for you right now.

Worry/Nervousness

With all the dread and anxiety that comes with growing numbers of layoffs, it's no surprise that many individuals worry about their employment. But this anxiety may quickly grow out of hand if you let it, and this can influence not just your mental health, but also your productivity, and your willingness to take chances at work.

Try these strategies to cope with worrying:

Don't surround yourself with concern and anxiety — For example, if co-workers meet in the break room to gossip and discuss job losses, then don't go there and worry with everyone else. Worrying tends to lead to more worrying, and that isn't helpful for anybody.

Try deep-breathing exercises — This helps calm your breathing and your heart rate. Breathe in gently for five seconds, then breathe out slowly for five seconds. Focus on your breathing, and nothing else. Do this at least five times.

Focus on how to improve the situation – If you dread getting laid off, and sit there and worry, it generally won't help you maintain your job. Instead, why not create methods to bring in additional business, and demonstrate how important you are to the company?

Write down your problems in a worry log - If you notice that anxieties are swirling around within your thoughts, write them down in a notebook or "worry log," and then set a time to deal with them. Before that moment, you may forget about these problems, knowing that you'll deal with them. When it comes to the time you've booked, undertake a thorough risk analysis around these items, and take whatever activities are required to reduce any risks. When you're scared and apprehensive about something, it might affect your self-confidence. Read our article on Building Self-Confidence to make sure this doesn't happen. Also, don't allow your anxieties to get in the way of being suitably forceful.

Anger/Aggravation

Out-of-control fury is possibly the most harmful emotion that individuals feel on the job. It's also the feeling that most of us don't manage very well. If you have difficulties regulating your anger at work, then learning to regulate it is one of the finest things you can do if you want to maintain your job.

Try these strategies to calm your anger:

Watch for early symptoms of rage — Only you know the danger indicators when anger is growing, so learn to detect them when they begin. Stopping your anger early is crucial. Remember, you can choose how you respond in a circumstance. Just because your initial reaction is to get furious doesn't imply it's the best answer.

If you start to become irritated, stop what you're doing — Close your eyes, and do the deep-breathing technique we discussed before. This pauses your furious thoughts, and it helps put you back on a more optimistic road.

Picture yourself when you're furious – If you visualize how you appear and act when you're upset, it offers you some perspective on the issue. For instance, if you're going to yell at your co-worker, consider how you would seem. Is your face red? Are you flailing your arms around? Would you want to work with someone like that? Probably not.

Dislike

We've probably all had to work with someone we don't like. But it's crucial to remain professional, no matter what.

Here are some strategies for dealing with someone you dislike:

Be courteous - If you have to work with someone you don't get along with, then it's time to lay aside your pride and ego. Treat the individual with decency and respect, as you would treat anybody else. Just because this individual acts in an unprofessional way, it doesn't indicate you should as well.

Be aggressive - If the other person is unpleasant and disrespectful, then strongly explain that you refuse to be treated that way, and peacefully leave the situation. Remember, set the example.
To learn more about addressing dislike in the job, please visit our articles on Working With People You Don't Like, Dealing With Difficult People, and Egos at Work.

Disappointment/Dissatisfaction: Dealing with disappointment or unhappiness at work may be challenging. Of all the emotions you could experience at work, these are the most likely to affect your productivity. If you've recently had a significant disappointment, your energy will probably be low, you may be reluctant to take another risk, and all of that may hold you back from attaining.

Here are some proactive strategies you may take to deal with disappointment and unhappiness:
Look at your thinking - Take a minute to recognize that things won't always go your way. If they did, life would be a straight path instead of one with hills and valleys, ups and downs, right? And it's the hills and valleys that frequently make life so exciting.

Adjust your target - If you're dissatisfied that you didn't attain a goal, it doesn't indicate the goal is no longer accessible. Keep the aim, but make a slight tweak — for example, extend the deadline.

Record your ideas – Write out precisely what is making you miserable. Is it a co-worker? Is it your job? Do you have too much to do? Once you identify the issue, start exploring ideas to address it or work around it. Remember, you always have the capacity to modify your circumstances.

Smile! – Bizarre as it may seem, plastering a grin – or even a grimace – onto your face may frequently make you feel pleased (this is one of the strange ways in which we humans are "wired").

www.ingramcontent.com/pod-product-compliance
Lightning Source LLC
LaVergne TN
LVHW050346160826
845677LV00014B/3823

9798846096400